God's Plan
for Everybody

Published by:

Associated Bible Students
6324 Tutbury Lane
Troy, MI 48098
USA

www.bibletoday.com

ISBN: 978-1-4675-8880-5

Printed in the United States of America

Introduction

This book has been written for children 6 years old and older. It is a Bible story book that begins with the creation of all things and attempts to explain, through simple words and illustrations, the great truths of the Bible and God's Plan for all people. It is a compilation of individual lessons created to guide a Sunday School class through the basic stories and doctrines taught in the Bible.

This book assumes the position that the Bible is God's Inspired Word and that it is correct historically, scientifically and morally. We believe that the great truths contained in the Bible are a guide for life, not only for children but for all people. 2 Timothy 3:16, 17

The Bible contains a theme of redemption for all who have ever lived. It promises deliverance from the great curse of sin and death that rules the world and our lives today. John 3:16

It considers all people precious before their Creator, who has done everything imaginable to provide for their ultimate peace and happiness.

It traces the fall from perfection of our parents, Adam and Eve, in the Garden of Eden when they disobeyed God. It then foretells the return, through Jesus Christ, of earth's inhabitants to the finished Garden of Eden which will encompass the whole earth.

It creates hope and encouragement that this present evil world will come to an end in due time – that God's will truly will be done on earth as it is done in heaven.

We pray the Lord's blessing on these endeavors.

Associated Bible Students, 2016

Table of Contents

THE OLD TESTAMENT

THE NEW TESTAMENT

God's Plan
for Everybody

Old Testament

When God was Alone

In the very beginning, before there was anything, anywhere, there was God.

And God was all alone.

There never was a time when God began. He was always here.

We don't really understand how that could be. But, we know it is true.

We don't know what God looks like. We only know for sure that He lives in light that is so bright no one could look at it, or even get close to it. 1 Timothy 6:16; Proverbs 8

God has a Son

God did not want to be alone. He wanted to have someone else like Himself to be with. He wanted a Son. So, He created a Son. He named His son the Logos, which means The Word. This may seem like a strange name. But it means that God's Son is the one who explains God, He is the one who is like God. He is God's only begotten Son, the firstborn of all creation.

You may wonder who was the mother of God's Son. Well, no mother was needed. God doesn't need any help to do whatever He wants to do. Colossians 1:15-17; John 1:1-4, 18; Revelation 3:14

Angels are Created

After God had His Son, He let His Son continue to make everything else that God wanted to make.

There are other beings God, with His Son, made. They are called the angels.

Angels are beings that are invisible. We call them spirit beings. They have bodies but they are spirit bodies. We don't know what their bodies look like. We cannot see them, even though they can be right next to us. But they can see us, and they can see God, and the Logos, and all the other angels. Angels do not die as we do. 1 Corinthians 15:40; John 1:1-3; 3:6-8; Colossians 1:16

Next came the Universe

After God and the Logos created the other spirit beings, the angels, They made the heavens and the earth.

By the heavens we mean the whole universe of stars and planets and space.

It may seem strange to think that there was not always a universe. But there was a time before the stars, planets, or any part of the universe were created. Genesis 1:1

Our Solar System Created

While God and His Son were creating the universe, they were also creating the part of the universe where we live — the earth.

The star we know best is our own sun, which is the center of our solar system. Genesis 1:1

The Earth Created

The next thing to do was to make the earth. When God, with His Son, made the earth it looked nothing like it looks now. It had no shape. All the ingredients that went to make the earth were made already. But God was just starting to put them together for us to live on it.

It's as if you were making a cake but all of the ingredients were laying all over the kitchen, and you had not even started to put them together yet.

We only know about how the earth was made because God tells us Himself in the Bible, in the book of Genesis. Genesis 1:2

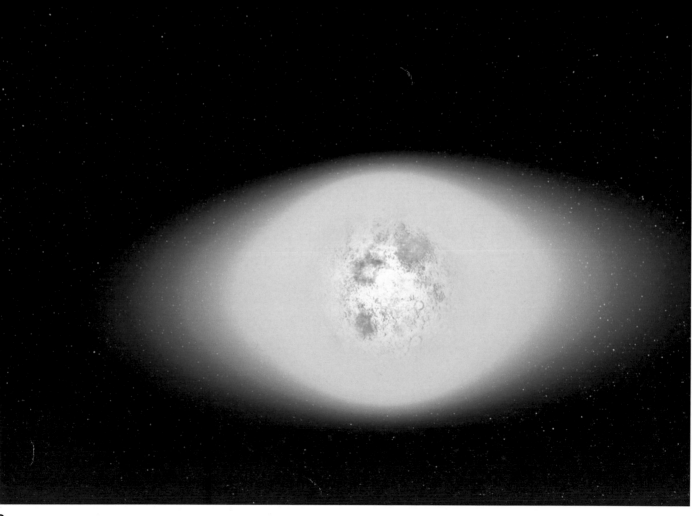

The Earth was Dark

God tells us in His History book, the Bible, that the earth was empty and dark. There was no life and there was no light. It was like the other planets that have not been finished yet. The earth is the first planet that God decided to finish. Genesis 1:2

Let there be Light!

The first thing God decided to do was to make light and darkness. He did not have to create darkness, but He did have to create light on the earth.

He did that on the first day. God's days are not the same as our days. They are much longer. The time it took to make light and darkness on the earth is called a day.

We know God does not look like a man. But we draw Him as a man so we can imagine what He is doing.
Genesis 1:4, 5

Water & Air

The next thing God did was make Water and Air. This is one thing that makes the earth different from any other planet. We can breathe air. We don't have to wear space suits! That's a wonderful thing.

At first the Air and Water were all mixed up together, so the earth was sort of a steamy swamp. When the Water fell to earth from the Air it created the oceans. The whole earth became one huge muddy ocean. Genesis 1:6-8

Water on top of Air

When God made the air around the earth some of the water fell to earth. But some stayed above the air, so the earth was floating in something like a bubble in space. The water that stayed on top of the air was probably like clouds getting ready to rain. Genesis 1:6-8

Water & Land

On the third day God decided to take the swampy mud and turn it into dry land and oceans. This was the beginning of the land and oceans we know today. He called the land "earth" and the water He called the "sea."

Remember that the land was empty, like a desert, with no plants or trees.

Stop and imagine what that must have been like if you stood on the empty earth. It probably was like standing on the moon! Genesis 1:9, 10

Water & Land

Grass & Trees

But it didn't last that way for long. Later on that day God made the grass and the trees. He also made all the seeds so the plants and trees would keep planting themselves every year. He made all the flowers, fruits and vegetables.

He was getting ready so when animals were created they would have plenty to eat.

Imagine how different the earth would look, compared to the empty desert! Genesis 1:11-13

The Sun & the Moon

Now here is a big surprise. The next day God made the Sun and the Moon. You probably thought He had done that already. Well, they were already made when God made the universe, but, He made them to appear on the earth at this time. So, the seasons, months and years began.

Because of the bubble of water around the earth you could not see the Sun and the Moon very clearly before this. So now you could see when the Sun would rise and He called that "daytime." When it would get dark and you could see the Moon He called that "nighttime."

He began the day with the nighttime and ended that day with the daylight. That was the end of the 4th day of Creation. Genesis 1:14-19

The First Fish

Now we begin the 5th day. Imagine the oceans with no fish, or frogs, or dolphins. In fact, they were completely empty — unless there were plants, of course.

God started making everything you can think of that lives in the water.

Look at the picture on this page. See if you can think of the names of the different sea creatures. These were all made on the 5th day. Genesis 1:20-23

The First Animals

Imagine what it would be like to start thinking of which animals to make. What would be the very first animal you would make?

From the smallest insect to the biggest animal, these were all made on the 6th day.

And look at all the animals in our picture. They are all friends. They are not fighting or trying to eat each other. All the animals were friends. They all lived together and ate grass or fruit. There was plenty of food for all of them. Genesis 1:24-31

The First People

After God had made all the different animals, and birds, and insects there were still no people. Imagine what it would be like to have a whole world filled with animals but no people.

God tells us how He made the first man. He made his body from the dirt. He put air into his lungs and his heart began to beat. He didn't make the first man and woman at the same time. He made the man first. And He gave him a name, Adam. He did not make a baby. He did not make a little boy. He made a grown up man.

Genesis 1:27, 28

Adam & the Animals

God did not make a baby because there was no one to take care of a baby. He made the first man a grown up so he could take care of himself, and the animals, and the earth.

God took a place on the earth and made it into a beautiful garden. That's where He put Adam. That was where Adam lived. Adam took care of the garden, and all the animals in the garden were like his pets. And he had names for all of them. And they were all friends.

Genesis 2:1-20

What did Adam Eat?

God had planted lots of fruit trees in the garden so that Adam would have plenty to eat. He did not have to worry about where to find enough food, and he never had to be hungry. He had lots of different flavors to enjoy from all the different kinds of fruit.

God gave the garden a name. He called it "the Garden of Eden." It was so beautiful, it was a paradise. Adam's job was to live in it and take care of it. Genesis 2:16

Adam got lonely

Adam had plenty to eat. He had a visit from God every day. He had lots of pets. And all of the animals had mates. But, he had no other person to be his friend. He was the only person in the world! Imagine if there were no other kids, or any people at all, to talk to.

God could see that Adam was lonely. That's what God was waiting for. He made Adam a mate as well. Genesis 2:20

God created Eve

Instead of making another body for Eve from the dirt, God decided to take part of Adam to make Eve. So He made Adam fall asleep and He took one of his ribs and made her from that. This was the very first operation!

When Adam woke up he saw Eve. And he loved her right away! She was so beautiful and perfect.
Genesis 2:21-25

Adam & Eve

When Adam woke up he saw the lady that God had made for him. He called her name Eve. He was so happy. She was perfect. She really was made just for him.

God told them they could eat all they wanted of any of the fruit on any of the trees, except for one particular tree. He showed them that tree and told them not to eat the fruit from that tree. He warned them that if they did eat that fruit, they would die.

They had never seen anything die, but they knew it was a bad thing. Genesis 2:17

God Rests

That was the end of the 6th day. God had alot more work to do. The earth wasn't finished yet. He had only finished the Garden of Eden. But he decided to rest during the 7th day. All the animals and the people on the earth were happy. No one was fighting. There was plenty of food. And no one was going to die. They were all made to be perfect. Genesis 2:1-3

Eve & the Snake

One day, while Eve was by herself, she was near the tree that they were not allowed to eat from. She saw there was a snake in that tree. The snake was eating some of the fruit.

She was surprised because she thought the snake would die. But, the snake did not die. The snake saw that Eve was watching him. So, he started to talk to her. It must have been a surprise to have a snake start talking to her. The snake told her the fruit was really good. He invited her to try a piece. She knew she was not supposed to eat it, but she wondered what it would taste like. Genesis 3:1-7

Eve eats the fruit

The snake made the fruit look so delicious. The snake told her it not only tasted good but it would make her really, really smart. She would start to know things she didn't know yet.

The snake told her that the only reason God did not want her to eat the fruit was because she would become more like Him. She would understand things that only God understood. She would know things both good and bad. Now she only knew about things that were good. She probably felt indignant that God was keeping secrets from her and Adam. So, she took the fruit and tasted it. She didn't feel any different. Genesis 3:6

Eve gives Adam a taste

Eve decided to go get Adam and have him taste the fruit. They shared everything. They had no secrets from each other. So, she wanted to run and tell him about her new discovery.

As soon as Adam heard Eve say she ate of the fruit he was upset. He knew she was going to die. He didn't want to be without her again. She meant everything to him. He loved her more than anything else. So, he decided to eat the fruit with her so they could be together. But when he ate the fruit he felt very bad. He knew he had done something wrong. For the first time he felt guilty.
Genesis 3:6

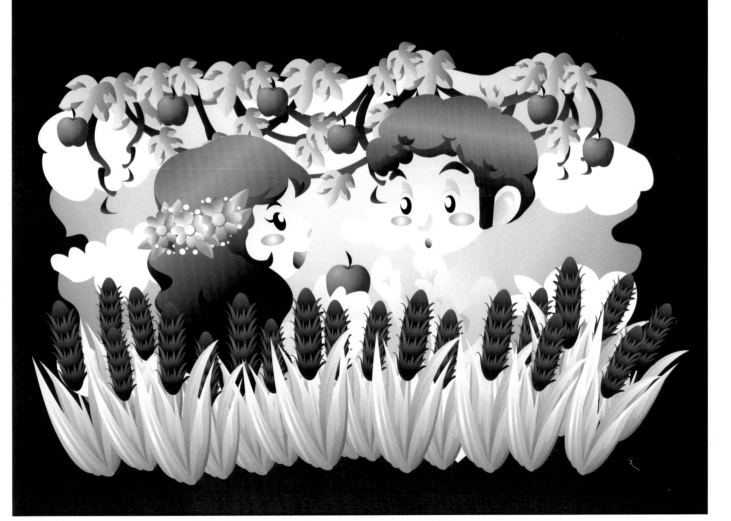

Adam & Eve Hide

Adam and Eve wanted to hide from God what they did. But God knows everything we do so that's not possible. When God came to visit them that day they were hiding. Of course, God knew where they were hiding and found them. He asked them why they were hiding. They said it was because they had no clothes and they were embarrassed. That had never been a problem before, but now they felt guilty so everything was different.
Genesis 3:7

God was very Angry

God asked Adam and Eve how they knew they were naked. They didn't know that before. They never wore any clothes. They told God they had tasted the fruit from the tree God had forbidden. And they felt guilty and embarrassed. That was a new feeling. They had never felt that way before. They told God the snake had given them the piece of fruit to eat and they had tasted it. God was very angry with them, and with the snake. Genesis 3:8-19

Who was the snake?

It seems very strange that a little snake could cause so much trouble. But it really wasn't just a snake. It was Satan.

We haven't learned about Satan yet, so let's talk about who Satan is. Revelation 20:2

The snake was Lucifer

To understand who Lucifer or Satan is let's go back to when God and the Logos created the angels. Remember that angels do not have bodies like we have. They have spirit bodies. They are like the wind. You cannot see them but they can come and go as they please. John 3:8

The first angel God and His Son created was Lucifer. He was a beautiful creation. He was admired by all the other angels. Ezekiel 28:13-15

Lucifer rebels

But, Lucifer was jealous of God and His Son. He wanted to be greater and to have more power. He wanted to be like them. So he became rebellious. That means he no longer did the things that God wanted him to do.

Lucifer wanted to be the ruler of the new planet God had made, the earth.

God knew what Lucifer was thinking. God always knows what we are thinking.

The name "Lucifer" means "son of the morning." But when he rebelled he became the prince of darkness, Satan.
Isaiah 14:12-15

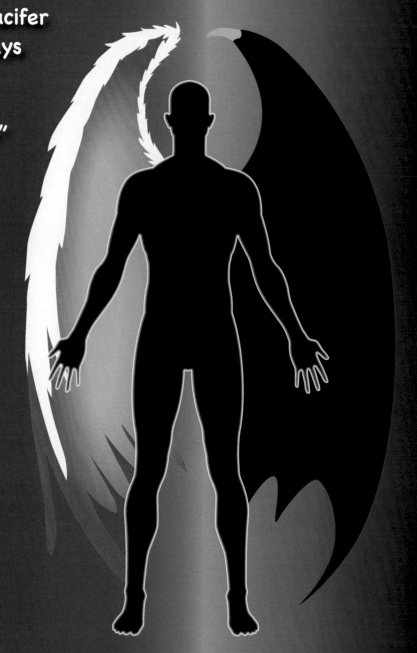

Satan falls from Heaven

Since God lives in light that is so bright no darkness can stay near it, Satan had to leave.

He could not be close to God any longer. He could not be near the Logos or near any of the angels that could stay in the light. Light and Darkness are opposites.

When Satan fell from Heaven, he fell down to the earth. Ezekiel 28:16

Satan talks through a serpent

Satan wanted to make Adam and Eve listen to him instead of to God. He knew that they talked with God every day. He could not let them know who he was or he knew they wouldn't listen. So, he decided to talk through a serpent. He knew Adam and Eve thought the serpent was very wise.

Genesis 3:1

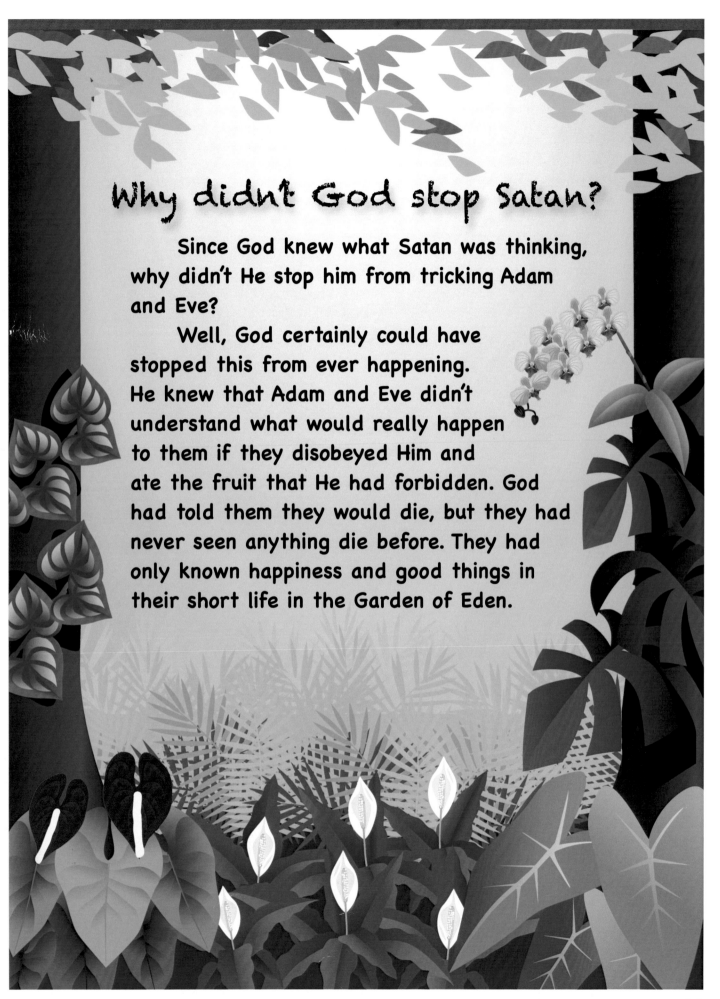

Why didn't God stop Satan?

Since God knew what Satan was thinking, why didn't He stop him from tricking Adam and Eve?

Well, God certainly could have stopped this from ever happening. He knew that Adam and Eve didn't understand what would really happen to them if they disobeyed Him and ate the fruit that He had forbidden. God had told them they would die, but they had never seen anything die before. They had only known happiness and good things in their short life in the Garden of Eden.

God knew Adam & Eve needed to learn...

God knew they needed to learn how important it is to obey Him, and not to rebel against Him as Satan had done.

So, He allowed Satan to lead them to being rebellious. Satan really didn't trick them, did he? They knew they were not supposed to eat the fruit from that tree. But they did it anyway. So God made them leave the beautiful place of Eden and go out to the rest of the earth that God had not yet finished. 1 Timothy 2:13, 14; Genesis 3:22-24

The Garden of Eden was closed...

God knew that as long as Adam and Eve stayed in the Garden of Eden they would live forever, because the trees of life would give them life as long as they ate their fruit. So, He put an angel by the entrance to the garden so they could not get back in. Genesis 3:24

The First Baby is born!

Adam and Eve had to make a home outside of the Garden for the first time. After the wonderful garden with so much to eat whenever they wanted it, it must have been difficult to find enough to eat. They did not eat meat yet, so they needed to find enough wild fruits and vegetables to eat.

They had their first baby, a little boy. They named him "Cain." The name "Cain" means "spear." When God told Adam and Eve they must leave the Garden of Eden He also told them that the child of the woman would bruise the serpent's head. They probably thought their son Cain was the one who would do that, so they named him "spear."
Genesis 3:15; 4:1

36

The First Little Brother

As time passed, Adam and Eve had another little boy, and they named him Abel. The name Abel means "breath." He was another life given to them.

As the boys grew, Adam and Eve must have told them many times about their life in the Garden of Eden and how they talked with God every day as a friend.

When they left the garden God made clothes for them from animal skins. This was a lesson that a life would have to be given for their shame or guilt to be covered. They didn't eat meat yet, so they only killed animals to use their skins, and for a sacrifice.

Genesis 4:2; 3:21

The First Sacrifice

As Cain and Abel grew up they developed different talents. Cain was very good at being a farmer and growing fruits and vegetables. Abel became a shepherd and raised sheep.

They both wanted to offer a gift to God for their gift of life and for providing for them in so many ways. Each brought to the Lord something from their work. Cain brought fruits and vegetables and put them on an altar and offered them. Abel brought a lamb from his flock.

God was happy with Abel's offering and accepted it. Cain's offering was not accepted. It did not provide a life to be given. This would show he was sorry for his sins and knew he needed a life to be given to cover them.

Genesis 4:3-8

The First Death

Cain was very angry with his brother. He was jealous that God had liked Abel's sacrifice, but not the one he had made. He did not understand that God wanted faith, not what they could give Him. God wanted them to understand that if they wanted to be friends with Him again, their shame and guilt would have to be covered by another life, not by their gifts.

Cain killed his brother that very day. Genesis 4:8

Cain runs and hides

Cain knew he had done something really bad and he wanted to hide. God always know where we are so He spoke to Cain and asked him where Abel was. Cain said, "How am I supposed to know? I'm not responsible for him." But God knew Cain had killed him. He punished Cain by sending him away. Genesis 4:14

Cain is punished

Cain had to go away and live by himself. Adam and Eve had lost both of their oldest sons in the same day. Abel was dead, and Cain was gone. What a sad day that must have been!

Adam and Eve must have been very disappointed. Remember that they had hoped it was Cain that would bruise the serpent's head and open up the Garden of Eden for them again.

Even though the Bible does not tell us their names, Adam and Eve had many more children. They had girls as well as boys, so that their children could grow up, marry each other and have more children. That's the reason that all people alive today are relatives of Adam and Eve!

Genesis 4:11-17

The Angels Come Down

As more and more babies were born they grew up, they got married and had more children. The first family got bigger and bigger. First they became a village, then a city, then more cities. After many years Adam and Eve died, and no one else remembered The Garden of Eden and the snake, or Satan.

Satan saw that if he could get these people to follow him now, he could become ruler of the whole earth. But, he didn't want to be king over people that were going to die. So he got an idea. He would convince some of the angels to marry the women on earth and have children. The angels do not die, so he knew that their children would not die.

He was able to convince some of the angels to come down to earth and appear to people as men. These angels that looked like men married human women and had children. These children were now part human and part angel, and they were bigger and stronger than any other people. They became bullies and made everyone else obey them. They became rulers of the earth. They were called "giants."

These giants were very bad. Over the whole earth people became more and more evil. Everywhere people were fighting and cursing each other. God decided it was time to bring these giants to an end! Genesis 6:1-7

These Giants had to Go!

God knew that as long as these giants were ruling over the earth, people would just keep getting worse and worse. This was because their influence was very evil. He decided they had to be destroyed, and the human family had to start over again.

There was one family left that was not evil and who would obey Him. So, He decided to save them. He would tell them what He wanted them to do to save themselves and some of the animals on the earth. Genesis 6:5-7

God sent a flood

God decided to send a flood to drown all the people, the giants, and any animals. He told Noah and his family to build a big boat that could hold 2 of every kind of animal on the earth. God brought these animals to Noah and lead them onto this huge boat. He then told Noah and his wife, Noah's 3 sons and their 3 wives, to get on the boat. After they and the animals were safely on the boat it started to rain. It rained for 40 days. They stayed on that ark for a year before they and all the animals could get off the boat! Genesis 6:11-22; 7:1-24

Building Noah's Ark

The World was Brand New

When Noah and his family got off the boat the earth was completely different. It was completely empty. The first thing they did was pray and thank God that they had been saved. There was a rainbow in the sky. They had never seen a rainbow before, because it had never rained before!

God told them that every time they saw a rainbow they should remember His promise. He made them a promise that He would never again destroy the whole world with a flood. This promise still is true. Genesis 9:8–17

Whenever we see a rainbow in the sky God wants us to remember His promise — that He will never again send such a huge flood that all the living things on the earth would be destroyed.

The First World had Ended

That was the end of the first World. The earth was still there but it was empty. Noah and his family had to start over again. They had to build houses and plant vegetables and figure out how to live by themselves. For the first time, God told them they should start eating meat. Up until that time no one had eaten any meat, only vegetables and fruit.

1656 years had passed since Adam was created in the Garden of Eden.

Now Noah and his family started to settle in the New World. They had more children, and those children had more children and in time people started to forget about Noah and his great deliverance from the flood. They built bigger and bigger cities and taller and taller buildings. They started to forget about God and His promises. The biggest building was called the tower of Babel. God did not want people to stay together. He wanted them to spread out and settle the whole earth. So he gave them different languages to speak so those who spoke the same language would gather together and move off by themselves and settle new places...

Genesis 9:3; 11:1-9

Building the Tower of Babel

The First World

The World that Was

From Adam & Eve until the Flood

People scatter over the earth

So people started traveling farther and farther apart. People who spoke the same language stayed together and became tribes, and as the tribes got bigger they became different countries.

People forgot about the true God that saved Noah and his family from the flood. They started making statues of different animals and started to believe in these statues as their gods. They would pray to these statues and call them by the names of gods they believed in. But none of them was the true God.

There was one man that still believed in the true God. His name was Abraham and he lived in a city called "Ur." God started to talk to Abraham. He knew that Abraham believed in Him and had so much faith in Him that he would do whatever God asked him to do.

He asked Abraham to move away from the country where he lived because they worshipped these false gods. He wanted him to be separate so he and his family could worship the true God and be His people.

Abraham obeyed God and moved his whole family to another country where they could worship and obey the one true God. They did not want to pray to these statues or "idols" which were no gods at all. Genesis 9:9; 12:1-3

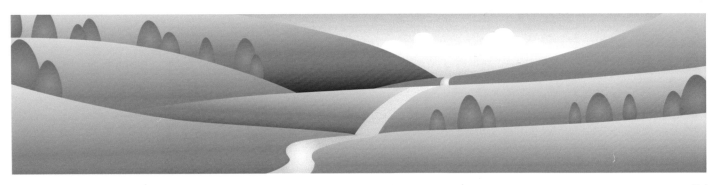

God's Promise to Abraham

God was very happy to see that Abraham did what He told him to do. Abraham believed God so much that he did not question Him and what He wanted him to do.

God told Abraham He would give him a son, and that through this son all the families of the earth would be blessed. Abraham was very happy about this because he had no children and wanted a son very badly. But a long time passed and he did not have a son. God waited a long time to give Abraham a son. He waited until Abraham was 100 years old, and his wife, Sarah, was 90 years old. By this time they had started to wonder if they would ever have a child. But God always keeps His promises.

They had a little boy and named him "Isaac," which means laughter. Genesis 17:1-19

Abraham Passes a Test

Abraham and his wife Sarah were very happy with their son. Remember, they had waited for many years to have a son of their own and they loved him as much as any parents could love their child. One day God asked Abraham to do something very hard. He asked him to take Isaac and sacrifice him to the Lord on an altar. He even told him what place to go to, to build this altar. He was to go to Mount Moriah. Abraham must have been shocked by this. This was the son God had given him when he was 100 years old. This was the son that Abraham thought was to bless all the families of the earth. How could God want him to do such a thing? Genesis 22:1-19

But Abraham knew God must have a good reason and he knew that God had the power to raise someone from the dead, so he started out on the journey to Mount Moriah with Isaac.

You can imagine how terrible Abraham felt as he traveled with his beloved son, Isaac. Isaac did not know what his father planned to do. He asked him where the animal was for the sacrifice. Abraham trusted that God would somehow make it all work out and said that God would provide the sacrifice.

When they reached the place on Mount Moriah where God had told Abraham to go, Abraham tied Isaac to the altar, which he had built out of stones. Isaac must have been willing to obey God as well, since it would have been easy for Isaac to run away.

Just as Abraham raised his knife to kill Isaac an angel from God stopped his hand. God saw that Abraham was willing to do anything God asked and did not make Abraham kill his son. Abraham looked up and saw a ram caught in a bush nearby and he sacrificed this animal instead of his son, Isaac.

It must have turned out to be a very happy occasion that day! This is an illustration of God sacrificing His only begotten Son, Jesus, for us. God had asked Abraham to do the very thing He was going to do. And the place where Jesus died was very close to Mount Moriah, where God told Abraham to go.

After this God repeated his promise to Abraham, that through Abraham and his son all the families of the earth would be blessed. He also promised Abraham to one day give him the land on which he traveled. He also promised him that he would have many more children, as many as the stars in heaven and as many as the sand on the sea. These were very wonderful promises, and remember, God always keeps His promises.

Age of the Fathers or Patriarchs

From the Flood until Jacob dies

Isaac, Jacob & Joseph

As time went on Isaac had two sons, Jacob and Esau. Esau did not care about the blessings promised for all the families of the earth. But, Jacob wanted the blessing. So he convinced Esau to sell his right as firstborn to receive this blessing from Isaac. Jacob also had children, 12 sons and 1 daughter. One of his sons was his favorite, Joseph. The other sons of Jacob were very jealous of Joseph and sold him into slavery in Egypt.

Slavery in Egypt was a terrible life. Joseph was beaten and put in prison, always longing to see his father and his family again. Eventually God let Joseph interpret a dream for Pharoah, the King of Egypt, and Pharaoh put Joseph in charge of all of Egypt. Since all of Egypt was going through a terrible famine there was no food anywhere. Joseph's family had to come down to Egypt to buy food. Joseph was reunited with his father and his family once again. And he was ruler of Egypt, helping his family get food during the famine.

Perhaps they thought in this way that one of the sons of Abraham would bless all the families of the earth as God had promised. But this blessing was to come in a much more dramatic way at a time still in the future.

Eventually Jacob died, then Joseph died, and a King or Pharaoh of Egypt was on the throne who did not like Joseph's relatives. He made them slaves and they had to work to build cities for him. He beat them and made them work very hard. Soon Pharaoh thought there were too many Hebrews that might overthrow his people. He said that all the boy babies that were born to them should be killed.

Genesis 25:19-28; 37 - Exodus 1

Moses is Saved

At that time a young mother had a little baby boy and he was very healthy and handsome. She thought that she could save his life by hiding him in a little boat that was hid in rushes along the river. The little boat floated into a place where Pharoah's daughter was swimming. She looked into the little boat and saw this beautiful baby boy and wanted to keep him. She named him Moses. Moses grew up as her son, as the grandson of Pharaoh, even though he was Hebrew, a son of Jacob, who also is known as Israel.
Exodus 2:1-10

Moses Grows Up

Pharaoh's daughter decided to adopt Moses and make him her son. But Moses' sister was watching what would happen to the little boat and ran to Pharaoh's daughter and asked if she needed a nanny to care for the baby. Of course, Pharaoh's daughter said yes and Moses' sister, Miriam, ran to get her mother. Moses' mother, Jochebed, raised Moses herself for the daughter of Pharaoh and taught him all about his family and his history of being a son of Abraham.

When he grew up Moses did not like seeing the members of his family being treated as slaves. He wanted to help to free them from being beaten and working so hard. One day he saw a man from Egypt beating one of his family members, a Hebrew slave. Moses killed the man and buried him in the sand. But, he was afraid he would be punished for this and ran away. He found a small tribe of people to live with in the desert and lived there for 40 years. He did not intend to go back to Egypt. But God decided it was time for Moses to return and help to free his people from slavery.

God spoke to Moses one day but He did it in a very unusual way. Moses was taking care of the sheep and he saw a bush that was burning. But, it never really burned up. It just kept burning. This was very strange. Moses watched the bush for a while and then he heard a voice speaking from the middle of the bush. Exodus 2:9-3:15

Remember that we cannot see God and we cannot see the angels or any spirit beings. We can only hear or see them when they want us to hear or see them. God had sent one of his angels to speak to Moses from this bush.

The angel was not a bush, and the angel did not look like a bush, or a fire. God and angels have bodies that we cannot see or understand. The voice from the bush told Moses that God had been seeing the slavery of His people, the Hebrews, in Egypt and wanted to deliver them. The Hebrews were God's people because they were children of Abraham. Remember that God had told Abraham that through his children all the families of the earth would be blessed. Without Isaac being born by a miracle of God, Abraham would have no children. So the Hebrew people were a miracle from God, God's people.

God was very angry with Egypt and with Pharaoh for treating His people so badly, and He wanted them to be freed. And He wanted Moses to be His servant to do this.

Moses Goes Back to Egypt

Moses was afraid to go back to Egypt and talk to Pharaoh. Even though he had grown up there he had changed very much since he had been in the desert for 40 years. He thought he would not be able to convince Pharaoh that he had spoken to God. He felt very weak. But God assured him that He would tell him exactly what to say, and that He would let his brother, Aaron, help him speak to Pharaoh. So, Moses went back. Exodus 4:1-20

God gave Moses a miracle to do in front of Pharaoh. His brother, Aaron, would throw his walking stick on the ground and it turned into a poisonous snake. Aaron did this in front of Pharaoh and told them that God said he was to let His people go. Pharaoh was not impressed with this miracle because his magicians did the same thing.

Moses does Miracles

Moses had another miracle from God. Aaron pointed his walking stick at the water of the river in Egypt and it turned into blood. Not only did the water in the river turn into blood but the water in the cups and pitchers in the houses also turned into blood. The people had to dig deep into the ground to see if they could find any water that was not blood.

But Pharaoh did not care about this miracle either because his magicians could do the same thing. This miracle lasted for 7 days. Pharaoh's magicians could do the same miracle somehow but they did not have the power to take it away. Only God, through Moses and Aaron, could take it away. Exodus 7:1-25

Moses does a Third Miracle

Now Moses still asked Pharaoh to let God's people go free. Pharaoh would not listen. So, Moses sent many more miracles which are also called plagues. The third miracle God sent through Moses was the plague of frogs. Aaron pointed his walking stick at the river and thousands of frogs came out and hopped all over the place. The people in Egypt could not eat, sleep, cook, wash or do anything because every place was over run with frogs. Exodus 8

But again Pharaoh's magicians could do the same miracle, so he was not going to listen to Moses.

Moses does a Fourth Miracle

For the next miracle God sent lice. If you've ever had lice in your hair you know how itchy it is and how hard they are to get rid of. And they are so small they are like dust. Aaron pointed his walking stick at the dirt on the ground and it all started to move and turn into lice.

For the first time the magicians tried to copy this miracle and they could not create lice. They didn't know how Moses could do it. They turned to Pharaoh and told him that this was truly the "finger of God." Exodus 8:16

The Fifth Miracle

For the next miracle God sent flies. You can imagine how bad it was to have flies crawling all over everything. We know how irritating it is just to have flies at a picnic, you want to swat them away from your food. You can't even sleep with flies buzzing around your head at night.

Pharaoh finally asked Moses to make the flies stop and he would let the Hebrews go. So Moses asked God to make the flies stop, but Pharaoh was very stubborn. Once the flies stopped he would not listen to Moses any more. So it was time for another miracle. Exodus 8:21

Something is Different

Up until now the people of Egypt and the Hebrews all had to live with the water that turned to blood, the frogs and the lice. But when the plague of the flies came God said he would make a difference between the people of Egypt and the Hebrews, His people. The Hebrews would no longer have to live with the plagues. The plagues would only be on the people of Egypt and their animals.

So, the Hebrews, and their animals, did not have any flies. There were more plagues that were sent. There was a plague of darkness, and it was only dark on the Egyptians. There was a plague of sicknesses. There was a plague of hail and locusts. Altogether there were ten plagues that God, through Moses, caused to come on the people of Egypt. Exodus 8:22-10:29

The Tenth Plague

But, the worst plague was the last one. The firstborn in every house was going to have to die. There was only one way to escape this time.

Each family had to take a little lamb and kill it and eat it. The blood that they got from this little lamb had to be painted on the door frame of the house to protect the house from this plague. Any house that had this blood on the door frame would be safe from this plague.

All the Hebrews did this and were safe. The people of Egypt did not listen. So, in every house, even the house of Pharaoh, there was someone who died. Exodus 11, 12

God's People are Free!

When Pharaoh's first born son died he sent a message to Moses in the middle of the night. He told Moses to tell his people that they should pack up their things and go and never come back! Wow! They had been in Egypt for over 200 years and now they were going to leave!

This news spread quickly. The Hebrew people packed up all they had, with their animals, and got ready to go. Their Egyptian neighbors gave them gifts of gold, silver, jewels, fine linen, and other valuable things.

They started traveling that very next morning. They spent all the next day meeting in one place so they could all leave together. By the next night they were all ready to go. God walked in front of them in a pillar of fire so they could see where they were going. During the day the pillar of fire turned into a cloud so they could all see it and follow it.

Soon they got to the shore of the Red Sea. By this time they had been traveling for 7 days. Pharaoh had been thinking about it and decided he wanted to chase after them. The more he thought about the plagues that had come on Egypt the more angry he became. He called together all of his soldiers and went after them on horses. The people thought they were trapped. Where could they go? Pharaoh and his army were behind them. The sea was in front of them. Exodus 12:31-14:14

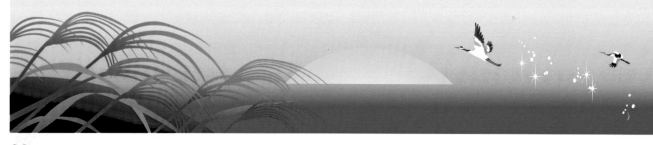

The Red Sea

   But then something wonderful happened. Moses lifted up his walking stick over the sea and it split into two parts, with a dry path going right down the middle so they could escape. They ran down the path and across the sea, with the water on both sides of them. It must have been frightening and exciting at the same time! The pillar of fire moved behind them to keep Pharaoh and his army from coming after them. **Exodus 14:15-31**

   When they reached the other side the pillar of fire moved and Pharaoh and his army ran after them through the sea. But God no longer kept the sea parted. He let the water flow back together. Pharaoh and all his army with their horses were drowned. What a miracle that was!

God's People are Delivered!

You can imagine how exciting that was. What a great deliverance Moses worked that day. Of course, it was God who did it. Moses stretched out his walking stick at just the time God was doing the miracle.

After all these miracles you can imagine the people must have thought that Moses was the Great Deliverer promised to Adam and Eve when they left the Garden of Eden. Remember, God told Adam and Eve that one of the children of Eve would bruise or hurt the serpent. He promised them that they would be able to escape the punishment of being cast out of the Garden.

But, Moses was not this great deliverer. He was a very great leader. But Moses told the people God would someday raise up a much greater deliverer than he.

The Ten Commandments

After they crossed the Red Sea the people were so happy they danced and sang praises to God. They had no doubt that God had delivered them from Pharaoh and slavery. Remember, there was a cloud that looked like a pillar of smoke that went before them. They followed this cloud so they would know where to go. At night it turned into a pillar of fire. Inside of this pillar was an angel of God leading them. God led them to the very mountain where Moses had seen the burning bush!

Moses climbed the mountain and God gave him the ten commandments or rules the people must follow. He gave them many other laws also. He also instructed Moses to build a place for the people to worship. It would be called the "Tabernacle," or Tent, of meeting between God and the people. Exodus 15:1-17; 19, 20

The Golden Calf

After all those miracles you would think the people would never forget God and all He had done to save them from Pharaoh and slavery. But, when Moses went up to the mountain to talk to God and get the Ten Commandments he was gone for a long time, over a month. The people got tired of waiting for him to come back down. They started to think Moses had died and was never coming back. So, they asked Aaron to make a statue, made of gold, of a calf.

Remember that this was one of the very things God did not want them to do: to worship or praise a statue as if it were God. This made God and Moses very angry. When Moses saw what they had done he threw down the pieces of stone the ten commandments were written on and they broke into pieces. **Exodus 20:23; 32:1-19**

VI
Thou shalt not kill

VII
Thou shalt not
commit adultery

VIII
Thou shalt not steal

IX
Thou shalt not bear
false witness against
thy neighbor

X
Thou shalt not covet

I
Thou shalt have no
other gods before me

II
Thou shalt not make unto
thee any graven image

III
Thou shalt not take the
name of the Lord in vain

IV
Remember the sabbath
day to keep it holy

V
Honor thy Father
and thy Mother

God Forgives

God forgave the people for making this calf but it had to be destroyed. Instead they built a special place where the people would come to God and be forgiven. It was called the "Tabernacle" or tent of meeting. This was the place where God would accept sacrifices and receive the worship and praise of His people.

During the day the same pillar of a cloud that the people followed would stand over the Tabernacle. At night the pillar of fire would also stand over the Tabernacle.

The people lived in tents and all their tents were set up around the Tabernacle. It was the center of their camp. Aaron became their first High Priest and God still spoke with the people through Moses and Aaron. Aaron would sacrifice the animals that were brought to God by the people. He would burn them on the altar where you see the fire. Exodus 40:18-38

The Walls of Jericho

The people were living in the desert around this Tabernacle for 40 years. When the cloud started to move they packed up their tents and went wherever the cloud went. When the cloud stopped they set up their tents and stayed there.

God gave them food to eat and water to drink. Their clothes and shoes did not wear out.

After 40 years it was time to go into the land God had promised to Abraham. So they had to cross the Jordan River. Once again God made the water of the river part so they could get across. By this time Moses and Aaron had died and they had a new leader, named Joshua.

They had to conquer the first city they came to, called Jericho. They marched around the city for a week. On the last day the walls of the city fell down and the city was theirs!

Joshua 1-6

Living in the Promised Land

After such a miracle the people must have thought that Joshua was the great deliverer promised to Adam and Eve. But Joshua was not that great deliverer. The name Joshua even means "deliverer." But the great deliverer or Savior promised by God to Adam and Eve was still coming.

Joshua lead them to conquer many more cities and they were able to start to settle the land and begin farming and growing their own food. God no longer had to give them food to eat as He did in the desert because they now could have gardens and farms and settle down to take care of their crops.

But the other people living in the land worshipped statues and idols. Very often they tempted the Hebrew people to do the same thing. They were no longer called the Hebrews but now started to be called the people of Israel. Israel was another name for Jacob, their ancestor, the son of Isaac, and grandson of Abraham.

When the people of Israel would forget about the true God who brought them to the land, and began to believe in other gods who were really demons, it made God very angry. Demons are the angels who fell to earth before the flood and had children who were giants in the earth. Their children, the giants, had died in the flood, but the evil angels were still able to deceive people. They would pretend to be gods and convince the people they should believe in them.

When the people of Israel would start to believe in these other gods who are false, God would punish them in different ways. One way God would punish them was by sending armies of their enemies to fight against them. When they would lose these battles often their enemies would make them work for them as slaves. They would take their crops and animals as their own and force them to work for them. When this would happen the people would start to pray to the real God once again for help.

Gideon

When the people of Israel would start to pray to the real God once again and ask for His help He would always hear their prayers and answer them. He would send a leader to help them fight against their enemies. One of these leaders was Gideon.

An angel appeared to Gideon and told him to take an army and sneak up on the Midianites, the enemies, at night. There were only 300 men but each one carried a burning torch. They carried a pitcher made of pottery over the fire to hide it. When they smashed the pitchers the fire burned brightly. The Midianites all woke up suddenly and started to kill each other. So, Gideon and his army chased them all away and Israel was free from them. Judges 6, 7

Samson

After such a deliverance the people must have thought Gideon was the Seed of the woman who would bruise the serpent's head and deliver them from death. But, Gideon died and the people once again started to believe in false gods.

Another deliverer God used was Samson. And this time the enemies were called the Philistines. Samson was very, very strong. When he was going to be born an angel told his parents he was never to cut his hair as long as he lived and he would stay strong.

But Samson had a girlfriend who was a very bad woman. She wanted to know why Samson was so strong. She really was not interested in Samson. She wanted him to be captured by the Philistines so he could no longer help Israel. Samson told her that the secret to his great strength was in his long hair, he had seven braids. If his hair was cut he would lose his great strength.

At night after he had fallen asleep she cut off his hair. She had told the Philistines to be ready to capture him.

Samson Captured

When they captured Samson they were very cruel to him. They put out his eyes so that he would be blind. Then they used him like an animal to grind grain for them. He spent his days pushing a wheel to turn a millstone. After being so strong and free it must have been very terrible to be blind and weak and a slave.

One day the Philistines were having a big party in a big arena. They were all drunk and wanted some entertainment. They decided to bring Samson into the arena so they could make fun of him.

By that time his long hair had begun to grow back. He prayed to God to help him one last time to get a victory over his enemies and the enemies of God's people. He asked to be lead to the pillars that held up the great arena. The young boy who was leading him did as he asked.

He used what strength had returned to push down these great pillars and kill everyone in the arena, including himself. This freed the people of Israel from the terrible Philistines.

David

After 450 years living in the promised land the people decided they wanted a king like all the other nations in the land. Up until now they had no king, only judges. These judges traveled through the country teaching the people what to do and how God would have them to live.

God was not happy that they wanted a king. God was their King. But he told Samuel, their judge, to anoint for them a king. To anoint means to pour oil on someone's head to show God had chosen that person for a certain job. Samuel found a young man named Saul and poured the oil on his head and he became their king. Saul turned out to be an evil king and God decided to replace him.

God sent Samuel to anoint another king in place of Saul. He was a young shepherd boy, named David.

David was a very strong and brave young man. He fought a lion and a bear to protect his sheep.

One day David went to visit the army of Israel fighting their enemies, the Philistines. He was amazed at what he saw. The Philistines had a giant soldier named Goliath standing in front of all the army of Israel, making fun of them, and making fun of God. He said that anyone who would come out to fight him would be killed.

David was horrified. He could not stand to hear Goliath make fun of the true God. He said he would go out and fight Goliath himself. Everyone thought he was crazy. He was just a young boy, he was not a trained soldier. He had no armor. He had no sword or other weapons.

But David was determined. He knew how to protect his sheep as a shepherd. He knew he had been able to fight a lion and a bear alone. 1 Samuel 8-17; Acts 13:20

He went to the king, Saul. Saul was still king and did not know that David had been chosen by God to replace him. Saul gave him his armor and sword to fight Goliath. But David was not used to armor and swords. He used his sling shot to protect his sheep. So, he told Saul and the other soldiers he would not fight Goliath using a sword and armor. He would fight him using his sling shot and the power and wisdom of the true God.

When Goliath saw this young boy coming to fight him with no armor and no weapons he laughed. He leaned his head back in laughter at this poor excuse for a soldier. When Goliath leaned his head back his forehead was exposed. David took his slingshot and hit him in the forehead with so much force Goliath fell backward. While Goliath was knocked on the ground David took Goliath's own huge sword and cut off his head! The Philistine soldiers were shocked. They all ran away. The soldiers of Israel ran after them and the Philistines did not come back to fight against Israel for awhile. 1 Samuel 17

Building the Temple

After such a great deliverance David eventually became king over Israel and ruled for 40 years. Towards the end of his life he really wanted to build a Temple for the worship of the true God. Remember the Tabernacle they had made while they were in the desert? Well, that's all they still had and it was hundreds of years old! David wanted to build a beautiful Temple instead.

God was very happy that David wanted to do this but he was a king that had fought many wars. He had killed many men in battle and God did not want someone like that to build Him a temple. So, He told David He would let his son build it. After King David died, his son, Solomon, became king over Israel and built a wonderful big Temple in Jerusalem, Israel's capital. 1 Kings 5

King Solomon

When Solomon, David's son, became king of Israel he had a very special dream. God came to him in a dream and asked him what he would like God to give him. King Solomon did not ask to be rich, and he did not ask to be powerful. He asked to have wisdom so that he could be a good king. God was very pleased with this request and made him the wisest king Israel ever had. 1 Kings 3:5-28

One day two mothers came to ask him a question. They lived together and both had a baby. In the morning one of the mothers woke up and found that her baby had died during the night. She took her dead baby and put him in the arms of the other mother, and took the living child for herself.

The other mother woke up and recognized that the dead baby she was holding was not hers. The living baby was hers. But the first mother claimed that the living baby was hers.

So they went to see King Solomon and asked him to decide which of them was the true mother. He told one of his servants to get a sword and cut the baby in two and give half to each of them. The real mother of the baby cried out and said the other mother could have the baby, only don't hurt him. Solomon then knew she was the true mother and gave the baby back to her.

News of his great wisdom spread through the world and he became very rich also. Kings and Queens would come to visit him and ask him all their difficult questions and bring him many wonderful gifts.

Surely the people of Israel must have thought that this was the great deliverer that God had promised to Adam and Eve, to Abraham, Isaac, Jacob, and Moses.

But in time Solomon turned away from God. Besides the wonderful temple he built for God he also built temples for false gods. He married many wives that did not believe in the true God but believed in false gods. They convinced him to let them worship their gods in Jerusalem also.

God turned away from Solomon and he lost his great wisdom. The people would have to wait before they would see the great deliverer, the seed of Abraham, come.

Many more kings came and died. Some were good kings and worshipped and believed in the true God. Many were evil kings who worshipped idols, statues, and false demon gods.

God would send prophets to warn the people of God's coming punishments for their rebellion.

Israel had kings for 513 years. Then God allowed Jerusalem and His great temple to be destroyed. All the people were taken as slaves and captives to Babylon and Assyria. It was a great tragedy.

Elijah & Elisha

One of the prophets God used to warn the people was named Elijah. Elijah was a very faithful servant of the true God. God sent him to warn one of Israel's worst kings, Ahab, not to worship false gods. But Ahab would never listen.

When it came time for Elijah to die God decided to take him in a very unusual way. He was to go with Elisha, his friend, across the Jordan River. Elisha knew that Elijah would be taken away that day. As they walked he asked if he could have Elijah's coat. Elijah told him that if he saw him go away he could have his coat. As they walked along they came to the Jordan River and had no way to get across. Elijah took his coat and hit the water of the river with it. The water split in two parts with a pathway down the

middle — just as it had for Moses at the Red Sea! Elijah and Elisha walked across. As they were walking together suddenly a chariot or wagon made of fire came out of the sky and separated them! Elijah dropped his coat and Elisha caught it. Elijah was swept away by the wind. What a shock for Elisha! Now he was alone. When he went back to the Jordan River he took the coat and hit the water and the river split in two once again! This time he walked across alone. From that time on Elisha was one of God's true prophets. 2 Kings 2:1-15

Jonah

Another one of God's prophets was not so faithful. His name was Jonah. God told him to go to a city named Nineveh and tell them to stop being so evil or He'd destroy their city. Jonah did not want to do that. So he ran way in the opposite direction! He got on a ship hoping to escape what God wanted him to do. Perhaps he thought God would just send someone else. But it's not a good idea to run from God. God sent a huge storm and the men on the ship were terrified. Jonah told them this storm was God's punishment on him, so they should throw him into the ocean. They threw Jonah into the ocean and the storm stopped right away.

God sent a giant fish to swallow Jonah so he wouldn't drown. He was inside that fish for three days and three nights. What a long, long time to be inside of a fish! But when God thought he had learned his lesson the fish threw him up onto the beach. Then Jonah was ready to go and do what God wanted him to do in the first place.

Jonah went to Nineveh and told their king that if they did not change their ways God would destroy the city. The

king listened to Jonah and told the people to repent. To repent means to stop doing bad things that God tells us not to do. The whole city changed their ways and they were saved!

Shadrach, Meshach & Abednego

Our next story takes place in Babylon, which is hundreds of miles from Jerusalem.

God's people had become believers in false gods and were punished. The temple was destroyed and all the people were taken as captives to Babylon. It must have been a very hard trip they had to make, walking the whole way.

Three of these were named Shadrach, Meshach and Abednego. They were young when they had been taken captive to Babylon. The king, Nebuchadnezzar, wanted these young men to be educated for important jobs he had for them. Eventually they were made officials in the king's government.

One day the king had a great big and tall golden statue put in a large square. He gathered all the officials from his kingdom and asked them to bow down to this golden statue. The three young Hebrews — Shadrach, Meshach and Abednego — refused. The law of God told them they must only worship the true God, no other gods or statues.

Nebuchadnezzar was really angry with them. They were taken before the king and given another chance. The king said that when he would have music played, they must bow down and worship this Golden Image of himself. Daniel 3

The Fiery Furnace

The music played and they would not bow down.

He threatened them that they must then be thrown into the fiery furnace. They said, "We know our God is able to save us from the fire. We don't know if our God will save us or not. But one thing we do know for sure is that we will not bow down and worship this golden statue."

This really made Nebuchadnezzar angry. He gave orders to heat the fire 7 times hotter. His servants tied up the three men and threw them in. Even the servants died from the heat while they were throwing them in. But the three Hebrew men did not die. In fact, the king could see them walking around freely in the furnace with a 4th person. The 4th looked like the Son of God.

The king was amazed. He brought them out and passed a law that all must worship the true God of the Hebrews!

Daniel

Our next story takes place in Medo-Persia. There were many others besides the three Hebrews taken captive at the same time. One of these young slaves was named Daniel. He was probably a teenager when taken captive as a slave. He was a very trusted servant of the king, Darius, and he gave him a very important job in Medo-Persia. But there were many evil men who were jealous of Daniel and wanted him killed. They did not know how to do it because Daniel was so honest and trustworthy they could not find anything wrong with him.

So they decided to trick the king into condemning Daniel. They convinced the king to pass a law that anyone who worshipped any other god besides the king would be thrown to the lions. Of course, Daniel worshipped the true God and would not stop praying to God so all could see. He was arrested and brought to the king. Then the king knew this was a trap. But, Daniel had broken the law and the king had to throw him to the lions. This was a terrible day for Darius who liked Daniel very much.

The Lion's Den

The day came and Daniel was put into the den with the lions. They had not been fed so they were especially hungry. But the lions would not hurt Daniel all night.

In the morning the king rushed to the lions' den and called Daniel to see if he was still alive. Daniel called back and said that his God had saved him and did not allow the lions to hurt him. The king was so happy! But he was furious with the evil men who had tricked him. So he brought them and threw them into the lions' den and the lions ate them all up. That was a great miracle!

Returning to Jerusalem

When Babylon was conquered by Medo-Persia the King, Cyrus, let all the Hebrew captives go free. What a wonderful deliverance! They had lived in Babylon for 70 years. Now they were allowed to go back to Jerusalem.

One of the first to go back was a man named Zerubabel. That's a big, long name. He started to build the Temple in Jerusalem that had been torn down by the soldiers of Babylon with King Nebuchadnezzar.

Two other men who went back were named Ezra and Nehemiah. Ezra was a priest and was in charge of teaching the people again about the law God had given to Moses.

Nehemiah was an official who worked for a later king, Artaxerxes. That's another big, long name. But he was very friendly to Nehemiah and put him in charge of building the wall around Jerusalem.

Once the Temple and the Wall were finished Jerusalem became a big city again. The Hebrew people, now called the Jews, started to have their own country once again. They had learned a hard lesson when they were slaves for other people.

They never again worshipped false gods or statues. They were very thankful to have their own land again and worshipped the true God in the new Temple.
Ezra 1

The Old Testament

Now it's time to review some of the things we have learned. We have talked about many of the things that happened during the time of the Old Testament in the Bible. The Old Testament talks about the time from the Creation of the Universe until the return of the Jews to Jerusalem, in Israel.

The first world on earth started when Adam and Eve were in the Garden of Eden. That world ended when God sent the flood to destroy it. The earth was not destroyed. But the way things were on earth was completely changed. The Bible calls that world "the world that was." 2 Peter 3:6

The second world started when Noah and his family came off the big boat they had built, after the flood. We are still in the second world on this earth. The ages begin and end but we are still in this second world. The Bible calls this world "the present evil world." Galatians 1:4

A new age also began at that time when God was special friends with certain people on earth. These people were those who had faith in Him. Noah was one of these people. Abraham, Isaac and Jacob were some others. We call them the "fathers" or "patriarchs." We call that age the "Age of the Patriarchs."

When Jacob died that age ended and a new age began. That new age was the time when God spoke with the children of Jacob, the Hebrews, the nation of Israel. We call it the "Jewish Age." That's why God delivered the Jewish people from slavery in Egypt. That's why He gave them His special law at Mount Sinai. That's why He brought them to Israel. That's why He sent them prophets to teach them. That's why He gave them judges and kings. But now in our reading we have come to the end of the Jewish Age when God considered only the Jewish nation to be His people.

On the next page we will draw a picture, or a time map, of what we have just talked about. Then we will go on to the next age, and the New Testament in the Bible!

Jewish Age

After Jacob died until Jesus was Baptized

Chart of the First Two Worlds....More to Come Later!

The First World
The World that Was
From the Garden of Eden until the Flood

The Second World
The Present Evil World
From the Flood until the Kingdom of Jesus Christ on Earth

The Age of the Fathers or Patriarchs
From the Flood until Jacob died

The Jewish Age
From Jacob until Jesus is Baptized

The Gospel Age
From Jesus Baptized until His Church is Complete

God's Plan
for Everybody

New Testament

The New Testament Begins

Over 450 years passed since our last story. The Jewish people continued to live in Jerusalem and to build more and more cities in the land of Israel.

Our next section begins the most wonderful part of our story. It is the story of how Jesus came to be born.

An angel came to a young woman, named Mary, to tell her she would have a son. She would call His name Jesus. This was a big surprise for her because she was very young and she was not married. But, she was happy to have a baby if that's what God wanted her to do. This was a great miracle because this baby would not have a father. God was going to be this baby's Father. This had never happened before.

Mary was engaged to be married to a man named Joseph. He would adopt the baby Jesus as his own. Matthew 1, 2

Mary & Joseph go to Bethlehem

As Joseph and Mary were traveling to Bethlehem, Mary knew she was going to have her baby that night. They looked for a hotel or some place to go that night, but there was no place that had any room for them. So, they had to stay in a barn! Can you imagine what it would be like to have a baby in a barn with animals all around watching? It must have been very strange but God was with them. The baby was born and laid to sleep in the nice, soft hay.

That night angels appeared to some of the shepherds who were in the field nearby to tell them about the birth of this miracle baby. They came to visit baby Jesus as soon as they heard the news! Luke 2

Jesus is Born!

These shepherds came to the barn where Joseph, Mary and the new baby Jesus were staying and bowed down to worship this little baby. The angels had told them that this little baby would change the world and bless all people.

Remember when God made Adam and Eve leave the Garden of Eden? He told them one of the children of Eve would bruise the serpent, the snake. This gave them hope that one day they would regain what they had lost because of the snake. They lost life, they lost the perfect Garden of Eden, they lost the visits they had had with God every day.

Well, Jesus, this baby, was this promised child. As we go on with our story we will see how this will be.

Wise Men Visit

Remember when Daniel was in Persia and he worshipped the true God there? Well, there were others who also started to study the prophecies because of Daniel. There were kings there who saw a star in the sky showing where Jesus was born. They decided to follow this star. They started on the long journey to Bethlehem with gifts for this new little King who was born. It took them a long time to get there, but when they arrived they gave Him three gifts. These three gifts were very precious. One of them was gold. One of them was frankincense, which is a very expensive perfume. And the third one was myrrh, which was also a very expensive perfume. These were wonderful gifts for a poor little baby, born in a barn with the animals. But God knew that little family would need these gifts for a trip they were going to take. Matthew 2

Simeon & Anna

When the baby, Jesus, was only 8 days old, Joseph and Mary took Him to the Temple. This was a law in Israel. The child was dedicated to the Lord and His service.

An old man was there to receive Him. His name was Simeon. God had told him that he would not die until he saw the Messiah. Messiah means "He who will save." It also means the one who is anointed by God. He knew immediately that this little baby was the One who would take away all the sin of the world. He was so happy to finally see Him.

There was also an old woman there named Anna. She also was so happy to see the baby Jesus. Think about how

happy you would be if you had waited all your life to finally see the Messiah, the true child of Abraham who would make all God's promises come true. Joseph and Mary must have been filled with joy and happiness when they left the Temple that day. What a blessing they had!

Luke 2:25-39

Joseph, Mary & Jesus Run Away

When the King, Herod, heard about baby Jesus and those kings who had come to worship Him he was very angry. He was afraid of any other king taking his kingdom away. So he ordered his soldiers to kill all the babies in Bethlehem. What a terrible day that was! But, baby Jesus was not there.

At night Joseph had a dream. In his dream God told him to take Mary and Jesus and go away to Egypt.

Remember Egypt was the place where the people of Israel had been slaves for over 200 years. Well, this would be a good place for them to hide. They got up in the night and hurried away before Herod gave his terrible orders.

We don't know how long they traveled but we know they stayed in Egypt until King Herod died.

After King Herod died Joseph had another dream. God told him to come back to Israel. He told him that those who wanted to kill Jesus were gone. So, they came back to Israel and went to live in a village called Nazareth.

Matthew 2

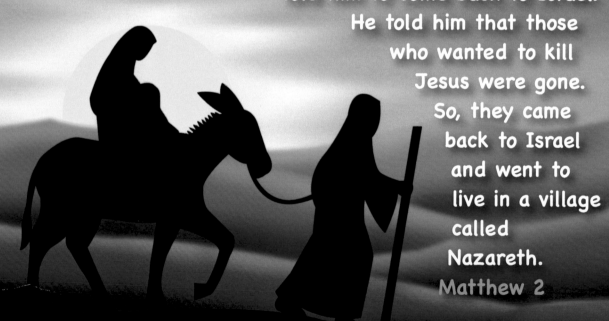

Jesus is Twelve Years Old

The next thing we read about Jesus is when He is 12 years old. He and His parents went to the Temple as they did every year. When His parent had left and were on their way home, they were with a group of people traveling together. They looked for Jesus in the group and could not find Him. They were very upset and returned right away to Jerusalem to try and find Him.

They looked everywhere they could think of and at last they found Him in the Temple, talking to the teachers and priests there about God's Word and the law of Moses. They were very upset with Him for frightening them so much and scolded Him for staying behind and not leaving to go home with them. Jesus was very surprised that they were upset. He thought for sure they would know He would stay at the Temple longer and try to learn more about His Father and His Father's will for Him. This was a surprise to Joseph and Mary, but Jesus left with them to go back home. Luke 2

Jesus is Baptized

After that we know that Jesus waited 18 more years before He decided to be baptized. We don't know anything more about His life except that he grew up and became more and more full of faith and wisdom and knowledge about God, His Father. Everyone who knew Him loved Him.

When He was 30 years old there was a man named John, who was His cousin, preaching at the river Jordan. He was baptizing anyone who was sorry for their sins. Baptizing means dipping someone in water. When they came out of the water it was a symbol of a fresh start.

John was very surprised that Jesus came to him to be baptized because he knew that Jesus was already very faithful to God and His law. He knew Jesus didn't have sins to repent from. He didn't need a fresh start!

After Jesus was baptized a dove flew down from heaven and John heard a voice saying, "You are my beloved Son and I am very pleased with You."

Can you imagine what it would have been like to be there that day? John 3:22

Jesus is Tempted

After Jesus was baptized He wanted to be alone with His Heavenly Father and spend time thinking and praying.

So He went into the desert for 40 days. During that whole time He was so busy thinking and praying He did not eat or drink.

Satan wanted to do what he could to tempt Jesus to follow him instead of God. He tried to get Jesus to do what he wanted instead of what God wanted.

One thing he wanted Jesus to do was take some of the stones and turn them into bread so He would have something to eat. This seems pretty harmless. After all, He hadn't eaten for 40 days! But Jesus would not do that, knowing it was what Satan wanted. He did not want to use God's power for Himself, only for others. Satan wanted Jesus to worship him. Of course, Jesus refused. Luke 4

Jesus is Tempted Again

Another thing Satan wanted Jesus to do was to jump off a high mountain so all could see that God would save Him. But Jesus refused to do this also. He knew that would not be what God wanted Him to do. God wanted Him to convince the people that He was the Messiah by His good works for them, not by being a magician.

Finally Satan knew that Jesus was not going to do what he wanted Him to do and he left. Then the angels of God came and helped Him and gave Him something to eat and drink.

Jesus goes to a Wedding

After 40 days Jesus returned home. There was a Wedding nearby and He and His mother were invited. During the Wedding reception they ran out of wine. This doesn't seem like a very bad thing but we must remember that wine is all they drank then. Imagine a Wedding Reception with nothing to drink. Mary, Jesus' mother, did not want the family to be embarrassed. So she told Jesus about it. Remember that He would not turn stones into bread for Himself. He would not use the power of God that He had for Himself. But He would use it to help others. So He went to the room where there were large containers of water. He turned that water into wine for the guests. This was the first miracle He did and from that time on people knew He had special power from God. John 2

Who is Jesus?

We know that Jesus had special power from God. We know He was born by a miracle. But Jesus wasn't just another great man. He wasn't just another prophet. He was the Only Begotten Son of God.

Remember at the beginning of our lessons we talked about when God was alone. Then He had a Son, and His Son was called the "Logos," or "Word of God." This Son of God was the baby who was born in the stable and was named Jesus. He was the mighty Son of God, sent to earth as a human baby, to be our deliverer. But, He wasn't just a human being like we are. He was perfect. He was not born as a sinner like we are. He was born without sin, just like Adam and Eve were before they disobeyed God. God decided before He even let Satan tempt Adam and Eve in the garden that He was going to send His Son down to save them, to deliver them from this punishment of sin and death. We think of Jesus as a shepherd and ourselves as the sheep He watches over. John 1:1; 1 Timothy 2:5; Hebrews 13:20

Jesus & His Apostles

The next thing Jesus did was choose 12 men to be His followers and to work with Him. They were called Apostles.

Jesus saw some fishermen in a boat on the Sea of Galilee. They had been fishing all night but had caught no fish. He told them to put the net on the other side of the boat. They did this and caught many fish, so many the boat was sinking. They knew this was a miracle.

When they brought all their fish to the shore Jesus told them to leave everything and follow Him. This took alot of faith to leave their jobs and their families and follow someone they did not know. But they were convinced by this miracle.

The names of these Apostles were Peter, Andrew, James and John. Peter and Andrew were brothers. And James and John were brothers. Luke 5:1-11; Matthew 4:18-22

The Lord's Prayer

As Jesus was teaching, His followers asked, Lord, teach us how to pray. So Jesus said that when you pray don't do it in front of people so they can see how much you pray. Pray from the heart, like this:

Our Father in heaven, holy be Your name. Your kingdom come, Your will be done on earth as it is in heaven. Give us today our bread for today. Forgive us our sins, as we forgive those that sin against us. Please do not abandon us in temptation but deliver us from the evil one. Amen.

Matthew 6:9-13

This is how God wants us to pray. He wants us to praise Him. He wants us to long for His kingdom to come on earth and His will to be done on earth, just like it is done in heaven, with the angels. He wants us to ask for forgiveness, and to be forgiving to others.

He wants us to want to be right and good. He wants us to realize we need help to fight against Satan. We cannot do this alone. Satan is too powerful for us.

Let us pray this prayer every day, in the name of Jesus.

Jesus & the Lame Man

Jesus lived sometimes in Capernaum, a city on the shores of the Sea of Galilee. One day some men brought a man to Him who could not walk. He had to be carried to Jesus on a mat. They all believed that Jesus could heal him if they asked Him to. Jesus was very happy to see how much they believed in Him and His power. He called this "faith." He said to this lame man, "Get up, take your mat and go home." The man got up and went home. The people that were watching were amazed. They praised God who had given such power to Jesus.

Jesus did many miracles like this to men, women and children. People brought Him whoever was sick and He healed many of them. It was a wonderful witness. People started to believe Jesus could be the promised one. Matthew 9:1-7

Jesus & the Blind Man

Jesus was at a nearby town called Bethsaida. Some people brought a blind man to Jesus and asked for Jesus to heal him. He took him by the hand and lead him outside the village. He spit on the man's eyes and put His hands on him. Then He asked him if he could see anything. The man said, "I see people and they look like trees walking around." Jesus put His hands on the man's eyes again. Then the man could see everything clearly. Jesus told him not to go back into the village but to go right home. Jesus did not want people to know about this miracle yet. He was afraid they would take Him and make Him their King, which is probably exactly what they would have done! The people wanted a King just like this who could heal them and raise them from the dead.

Mark 8:22-26

Jesus Feeds Them

They also wanted a King who could feed them. One day as Jesus was teaching over 5,000 people the time came when everyone was hungry and it was time to eat. But they had no food. Jesus' followers asked to see if anyone had any food. A young boy came and gave them all he had, 5 loaves of bread and 2 small fish. This was not very much to feed 5,000 people. But Jesus took these and made enough to feed everyone until they were full, and there was some left over! The Apostles were amazed. They had never seen anything like it. Now this was someone the people wanted to follow.

But Jesus did not want people to listen to Him just because He was going to heal them, or give them something to eat. He wanted them to love Him. He wanted them to love His Father. He wanted them to do His Father's will even when there was no reward for it. Matthew 14:13-21; Luke 9:12-17

Healed by Jesus' Robe

Jesus healed people because He wanted to and He had the power from God. But, He felt it every time He healed someone, or raised them from the dead. He felt some of His strength go from Him and He became a little weaker each time.

One day as Jesus was going to raise a young girl from the dead who had just died, Jesus suddenly stopped and looked around, and said, "Who touched me?" Everyone was surprised because there were alot of people touching Him. But Jesus could feel strength leaving Him, so He knew someone had just been healed.

A woman had touched Him who had been sick for many years. She had said to herself, "If only I can touch his robe, I'd be healed." And because she believed so strongly God blessed her and she was healed! Matthew 9:20-22

Jesus & Zacchaeus

One time when Jesus was in Jericho He was walking down the street, and there were many people who had come to hear Him teach. There was a man that was very short, named Zacchaeus. He wanted so much to see Jesus but he couldn't see over the crowd. He also was a man who collected taxes from people so no one liked him and probably didn't want to let him through. So, he climbed up into a tree to see Jesus.

Jesus knew people's thoughts so He knew how much this short man wanted to see Him. He stopped in front of the tree and spoke to Zacchaeus by name. Zacchaeus was amazed that Jesus knew him. Jesus told him he would be eating supper at his house that night. Zacchaeus became a follower of Jesus that day and repented of all his sins. He promised to give back any money he had collected dishonestly. Luke 19:1-9

Jesus Walks on Water

One night Jesus wanted to be alone to pray. So He told His Apostles to go out on a boat on the Sea of Galilee and He would meet them later. During the night there were large waves and it was very windy on the sea.

The Apostles looked out and saw Jesus coming to them walking on the water of the sea. They could hardly believe their eyes. Peter didn't even think about it. He jumped out of the boat and walked out to meet Him. But suddenly he realized what he had done and was terrified and started to sink. Jesus caught him and brought him back safely into the boat. Then the wind stopped and the sea was at peace. Matthew 14:22-33

Jesus & the Children

One day Jesus was teaching the crowds of people. There were little children who started playing with Him and sitting on His lap. The Apostles told them to go away, that Jesus was way too busy to play with them.

But Jesus loved children, just like He loved all people, and He wanted the children to be around Him.

He taught a lesson, that any one who wants to be a follower of Jesus must be like a little child. What does that mean? It means a follower of Christ must be humble and not think too highly of himself. It means they must be sincere. It means they must say what they mean and not be a hypocrite.

Matthew 19:14, 15

Jesus Warns the Apostles

Jesus started warning His Apostles that He was going to die. They could not understand why He would say such a thing. He was only 33 years old. He was their King. He was their Messiah, the chosen one of God. They thought He must not mean it. They thought He was somehow just kidding.

But Jesus was very serious. He knew He had to die soon. He had come to this earth as a human for this very reason. He was going to give His life in place of the life of Adam, who sinned in the Garden of Eden and made all of us, his children, die. Jesus said that just as the prophet Jonah spent 3 days inside the big fish, He would spend 3 days dead in the earth–but then He would rise again from the dead.

Matthew 12:40

Jesus' Feet are Washed

One day Jesus was eating dinner with His followers and a woman came into the room and started to wash His feet, and dry them with her hair. This was very surprising to the disciples. They wondered why Jesus let her do this. But she was a woman Jesus had healed and she wanted to show how thankful she was. She had demons cast out of her. Do you know what that means?

Remember back to our story about the flood. Angels had become men and married women, and they became very evil. Well, these evil angels were still causing people much harm. They would make people do things they didn't want to do and these poor people could not help it. So, this is what had happened to this woman. Jesus freed her from these terrible demons. These demons are still hurting people today. That's why we are to have nothing to do with witches or witchcraft because this is one way these demons work to hurt people. Jesus had power over these evil angels—and He still does.

Luke 7:37, 38

Raising the Widow's Son

Of all the miracles done by Jesus, the most fantastic miracle was when he raised someone from the dead.

One day, when Jesus was traveling through a city called "Nain," he saw a funeral procession, and a widow weeping over the death of her only son. He felt very sorry for her and turned to her and said, "Don't cry." He then went to the stretcher where her son was lying down and told him to get up. He suddenly sat up and started to talk!

Can you imagine how his mother felt that day? She was overjoyed with relief. Everyone who saw this great miracle was convinced that Jesus was a great prophet sent from God! Luke 7:11-17

We can just imagine that the enemies of Jesus did not believe this actually happened. They might say that this man really wasn't dead but was just sleeping and Jesus woke him.

The enemies of Jesus did not believe He was a great prophet sent from God. They thought He was a liar.

The enemies of Jesus were not happy for the people who were healed or raised from the dead. They were not happy Jesus was feeding the poor. They just wanted to get rid of Him because He was making them look bad by comparison!

Raising Lazarus

One day while Jesus was traveling a messenger came to Him and told Him that one of his friends was very sick. His friend's name was Lazarus. But Jesus did not go to heal Lazarus. He stayed away for 2 more days. Then, Jesus decided it was time to go to see Lazarus and his sisters. He told His disciples that Lazarus was sleeping. Really he meant that Lazarus was dead, but death really is like sleep. The person who dies is resting and knows nothing until they wake up. John 11

When Jesus got there Lazarus had already been dead and buried for 4 days! Martha, his sister, said, "Lord, if you had come my brother would not have died." Jesus told her that Lazarus would rise from the dead. Martha knew Lazarus would rise from the dead in the Kingdom of God, but she wanted him back right now! Jesus cried for Lazarus and his family and all the people who were so sad. He asked to be taken to the grave. As Jesus stood before the grave and prayed he called out, "Lazarus, Come Out!" Lazarus came out!! He was wrapped in grave clothes and needed to be unwrapped. But he was alive! No on could deny this miracle and many who saw this believed Jesus truly was from God!

Jesus Goes to Jerusalem

Jesus knew it was God's will for Him to die in Jerusalem. So He started going there. Jerusalem was the largest city in Israel. That's where the Temple was that had been built when the people of Israel returned from captivity almost 500 years before. As Jesus was going into the city many people started shouting His name and laying down branches from palm trees for His donkey to walk on. They shouted, "Blessed is the King of Israel! Blessed is He that comes in the name of the Lord." The priests and teachers at the Temple were very jealous of Jesus. They did not like that the people liked Him so much.

You would think that since He healed them, raised some from the dead, fed them and encouraged them, that they would be happy. But they hated Jesus and how popular He was. They started to think about how they might be able to kill Him. Jesus knew this, and He knew it was God's will for Him to soon die. John 12:12-19

Jesus Washes Their Feet

A week later, when the people were going to celebrate the Passover, Jesus and His Apostles were getting ready to also celebrate the Passover in Jerusalem. Remember our story of the Passover when the people of Israel left Egypt after the ten plagues? Well, the people of Israel still celebrated this anniversary every year at the same time.

Jesus and His Apostles were all together as a family for this very important night. Jesus had been telling them more and more often that He was going to die. The Apostles were very sad. They didn't understand why Jesus kept telling them this. They certainly didn't want Him to die.

Before they ate Jesus got up and started to wash each of their feet. They were surprised because this was the work of servants. Jesus was trying to teach them that they must all be servants for each other and take care of each other.

John 13:6

125

A Very Important Meal

After Jesus washed their feet they ate together. They still ate lamb like the Israelites did at the first Passover. But after the lamb Jesus did something very special. He took some bread and passed it around and had each Apostle take a piece. He told them they were eating His body. Then He took a cup of wine and passed it around and had each Apostle take a sip. He told them they were drinking His blood.

Do you think they were really eating Jesus' body and drinking His blood? Of course not, but it meant something very important. It meant that the followers of Jesus became part of His body and part of His blood so they were all like one body. He wanted them to understand that they were becoming part of Him, and part of His work.

This would be their last meal together before Jesus died. He asked us to do this every year to remember His death. The followers of Jesus still do this every year at the time of Passover.

Matthew 26:17-30

Jesus' Last Prayer

After they finished eating their last supper together they left the room where they were and went to the Garden of Gethsemane. It was a quiet place where Jesus wanted to pray to His Father. He knew He would die soon and He wanted to talk to His Father about it.

Before Jesus even came to earth to be born as a human baby He knew He was going to die. But it was still a very frightening thing. He wanted to be sure he had done everything God wanted him to do. He wanted to see His Father again more than anything else in the world.

He knew that if He had done everything His Father wanted Him to do He would be raised from the dead. He would be more glorious and powerful than He had ever been before.

But He also wanted to be sure He would be able to save all the people on earth from sin and death. That's the very reason He had come to earth as a perfect man in the first place!

As an answer to Jesus' prayers, God sent an angel to encourage Him. Matthew 26:36

Jesus Arrested

While Jesus was still praying in the Garden the soldiers from the city came to arrest him. One of the Apostles named Judas Iscariot had told them where He was. The priests and teachers from the Temple who were jealous of Jesus wanted to kill Him. Jesus went with them willingly.

He knew it was His Father's will. But the Apostles were confused and frightened. They all ran away and left Jesus alone. Jesus also knew this was going to happen. He had tried to warn them but they did not understand the Plan of God yet.

Jesus was arrested and lead to court by a group of soldiers. He had done nothing wrong so the priests and teachers had to make up some false charges against Him.

Jesus did not defend Himself because He knew He had to die in place of Adam.

Satan was His enemy and also wanted Him dead. God allowed this because it fit into His Plans all along.
Matthew 26:49

Jesus on Trial

The soldiers that arrested Jesus took Him to the High Priest and the other priests and teachers. You would think that since they were servants of God they would love Jesus. But they did not believe that Jesus was the Son of God. They thought He was just pretending to be the Son of God and lying to the people. They could not explain how Jesus could do such wonderful miracles, but they did not seem to care.

They brought Jesus to Pilate, the Roman ruler in Jerusalem. Pilate knew they were against Jesus because they were jealous of Him. He knew that Jesus had done nothing wrong. So, Pilate tried to save Jesus. But the priests and teachers wanted Jesus dead. They called out for Jesus to be crucified. They convinced the people to cry out for Jesus to be crucified.

The people were so angry Pilate was afraid that these people would cause a riot. So he agreed to send Jesus to be crucified.
Matthew 27:1-26

Jesus Carries the Cross

When someone is crucified their hands and feet are nailed to a cross made of wood. Jesus had to carry His cross made of heavy wood through the city of Jerusalem to the place where criminals were crucified. Jesus and two other criminals were going to be crucified that day.

Jesus was not a criminal. He is the Son of God. But the people and the priests did not believe it. They thought He was lying. And because they thought He was lying, they thought He deserved to die.

God knew this would happen. And God forgives those people for killing His Son. He knew Jesus was going to take the place of Adam. He knew He was going to die in his place, so that he and all his children could escape from sin and death. 1 Corinthians 15:21, 22

Jesus is Crucified

Jesus and the two criminals were crucified together. His mother Mary came to be there as He was dying. The Apostle John was there with her. Other followers of Jesus also were there. It was a terrible day for them. They were very confused. Even though Jesus had told them He must die, they didn't expect it. They were surprised and confused. They thought Jesus was going to be King, that He would set up a Kingdom and free them from the Romans and their laws.

But instead, Jesus was dying. He was going to free them from something much worse than the Romans and their laws. He was going to free them from sin and death. But first he must spend parts of 3 days asleep in death.

It was about 6 hours before Jesus died. When He died, a rich man named Joseph asked Pilate if he could take Jesus and bury Him in his own grave. Pilate gave Joseph permission to take Jesus' body away. Matthew 27:35-57

Jesus is Buried

As Joseph was taking Jesus' body away to bury it, many of His followers watched to see where they would take Him. They were not going to be able to prepare His body to be buried now because it was almost the sabbath. Remember when we read our story about the Ten Commandments? One of the Ten Commandments was to remember the sabbath day, to keep it holy. That meant that they could not do any work on the sabbath day. It was a special day of rest and worship. Matthew 27:55-60

Jesus died on Friday afternoon, at about 3 p. m. The sabbath started at about 6 p. m. They had just enough time to

see where Jesus was buried. Then they all had to hurry home to keep the sabbath.

It must have been a very hard sabbath day for them. They had not even had time to prepare Jesus for His burial after He was crucified. They were sad and confused. They probably spent that day together, trying to understand.

Jesus is Resurrected!

Early the next morning, Sunday morning, some of the followers of Jesus rushed to the tomb. They had spices and fresh linen to wrap up Jesus' body. But when they got there they saw the stone that was in front of the door had been taken away. They went in and saw that the body of Jesus was not there. Only the grave clothes were still there. And the clothes were lying in the grave still wrapped as they had been around the body of Jesus. But the body was gone! Then suddenly they saw an angel with shining clothes.

The angel told the women that Jesus was not there, but He had been raised from the dead. Then the angel told them

to go and tell the Apostles the news. The women were overjoyed! Can you imagine how they felt when they saw the angel and heard this news? They ran quickly to where the Apostles were gathered to tell them the news. But the Apostles found it hard to believe.
Mark 16:1-8

The Empty Tomb

As soon as they heard the news the Apostles Peter and John ran as fast as they could to see what the women were talking about. They did not see the angel but they saw the grave clothes lying there in the shape of a body and they believed that Jesus had been raised from the dead. It would be very convincing, don't you think, to see such a thing? Then they went back home.

But a follower of Jesus, Mary Magdalene, stayed at the tomb and she was crying. She did not understand yet that Jesus had been raised from the dead. She looked into the tomb and saw two angels in white, seated where Jesus' body had been. They asked why she was crying. She told them she wanted to know what had happened to Jesus' body. Then she turned and saw Jesus standing there and He said her name, "Mary." She recognized that it was Jesus. John 20:10-16

The Road to Emmaus

Later that day there were two other followers of Jesus who were walking on the road going to a town called Emmaus. A stranger approached and started to walk with them. He asked them why they were so sad. They were surprised He had not heard about the crucifixion of Jesus, whom they thought was the Messiah, the promised one.

Really this stranger was Jesus, raised from the dead, but they did not recognize Him. Jesus was not raised as a human being but as a powerful spirit being. He appeared to them in a body they did not recognize. Remember, He had given His life as a man in exchange for our father, Adam. He told them of

the many prophecies in the Bible that had come true. He told them of the prophecies that explained that Christ would have to suffer and die.

When they arrived at an Inn He broke bread with them. Then He vanished. They knew it was the Lord!

Luke 24:17-27

Jesus Appears

Later that Sunday evening the followers of Jesus were together with the doors locked. They were afraid they could be arrested for being His disciples. Suddenly Jesus appeared in the middle of the room and said, "Peace be with you." As you can imagine they were very amazed and overjoyed. He showed them the wounds in His hands where He had been crucified. Remember Jesus was now a powerful spirit being. He appeared to them this time in a body they could recognize. This was to help them believe it really was Him, raised from the dead. But there was one Apostle who was missing. His name was Thomas. When

Thomas heard that Jesus had appeared to them he did not believe it. He said that he would have to see Jesus himself to believe it.

A week later Jesus appeared to them again, but this time Thomas was with them. He asked Thomas to touch His wounds so he would believe it was He! John 20:24-29

Jesus Ascends

Jesus appeared to them eleven times during the days after His resurrection. Sometimes He appeared to them all. Sometimes He appeared to just one of them. Finally, 40 days after He was first resurrected, He was ready to go away to His Father. He was with His disciples when they asked Him if now He would establish His Kingdom and restore the nation of Israel. Jesus told them that the time for this was only known to His Father in heaven. Jesus did not know yet when the time for that would be. He told them to wait in Jerusalem until they had received power from God. Then, suddenly, He started to ascend. They could see Him as He rose up into the sky and then they lost sight of Him as He was covered by a cloud.

What a strange sight this must have been! Jesus wanted them to know they should not expect any more appearances.

They stood there until two angels appeared to them and told them there was no reason to continue to look up into heaven. So they returned to Jerusalem and waited.

Acts 1:4–11

Disciples Receive Power

Jesus' Apostles and His other followers waited in Jerusalem as He asked them to do. They waited there for 10 days. On the 10th day after Jesus had ascended they were gathered together. It was a day of a feast, called the Feast of Pentecost. Suddenly they all heard a sound like the wind fill the room. They looked and over each of their heads was a flame. This flame was a symbol of God's Holy Spirit. Remember that Jesus told them to wait for power. This was God's power being given to them so they could do the work God meant for them to do.

When they received God's power or spirit they could now understand what Jesus had been trying to tell them. They now knew what He meant when He said that they would become

fishers of men. They started to preach and then they discovered they could speak in different languages, even though they didn't know these other languages. This was just the first miracle they would find they could do. They now understood the work God had for them to do. Acts 2

Gospel Preaching Begins

The Apostles had thought it would be a simple matter for Jesus to set up His Kingdom on the earth. They had thought that the work of deliverance would begin for all the nations of earth, starting with Israel.

But they now understood that there was a very important work that had to be done before that could happen. Now they understood that Jesus was going to call out from all nations "a people for His name," those that would be followers in His footsteps. These would become His bride in heaven. These would work together with Him in setting up His Kingdom and would rule together with Him. So the work of witnessing and calling these followers from all nations would start immediately.

This is the work that has been going on ever since the Apostles started it that day. They started preaching, and we still are preaching this wonderful invitation. We invite whoever wants to, to become part of the Bride of Christ, to rule together with Him when He sets up His Kingdom on the earth.
Acts 2

The Apostles Heal

God knew that for people to believe the Apostles, to believe that Jesus had been raised from the dead, the Apostles had to have the same power Jesus had used. So, God gave them many abilities and powers. They were able to raise people from the dead, to heal the lame and the blind. They were able to speak in different languages miraculously. They were able to know what people were thinking.

One day Peter and John were on their way to worship and pray in the Temple. There was a man at the gate who was handicapped from the time he was born. He could not walk. When he saw Peter and John he asked them for some money. Peter said to him, "I have no money but I can give you what I have. In the name of Jesus Christ, get up and walk!"

The surprised man suddenly became strong and he was able to get up and walk for the first time. All the people who saw this miracle started praising God, because they knew he was there for many years begging. Acts 3

Peter Gives the Holy Spirit

As the Apostle Peter traveled and preached, he would baptize and give new Christians the gifts of the holy Spirit. It was one of the gifts the Apostles had – to be able to give the gifts to others. Everyone could not do this. One day a man saw the Apostle Peter laying his hands on someone and that person could suddenly speak a new language. This man's name was Simon. He had been a magician. He had amazed the people around him for a long time with his magic.

Simon wanted to have this power and thought he could buy it from the Apostle. He thought the Apostle was just a very powerful magician. He offered money to the Apostle for this secret. The Apostle Peter was very angry. He did not want anyone to think he received this power by magic! This was the power of God that had been given him. It was not for sale! So he turned and said, "Your money will perish with you!" Then Simon asked them to pray for him that he not be punished!
Acts 8

Saul Blinded

There was a man named Saul and he was a very important man among the Jews. He did not believe that Jesus had been raised from the dead. He thought the Apostles were lying and he wanted to stop them from preaching. He was on his way to a city called Damascus to stop the Christians from preaching there. On his way he saw a very bright light and was knocked off his horse. He also heard a voice which said, "Saul, why are you persecuting me?" This was the voice of Jesus. Saul asked who He was. He said, "I am Jesus, who you are persecuting." You can imagine how shocked Saul was. He thought he was doing the right thing to stop the Apostles from preaching.

Saul got up, but when he opened his eyes he could not see anything. He was blind. His companions led him the rest of the way to Damascus and when he got there he met a Christian named Ananias. Ananias healed his blindness and Saul became a Christian. God changed his name to Paul and he became an Apostle to replace Judas, who had betrayed the Lord. The disciples were very surprised that God had called Saul to be an Apostle! Acts 9

Paul Escapes

The people who had been friends with Saul, now called Paul, were very angry with him. They had all been together in persecuting Christians. Now Paul was a Christian himself! And he had had a vision. The Apostle Paul was now telling everyone about his vision. His old friends thought he had to be stopped.

They decided they would have to kill Paul. They stood at the city gates of Damascus to see if they could catch him. But Paul had learned about this and the other Christians decided they would help him escape. They found a large basket and lowered Paul down in it through the wall. So his enemies did not succeed in catching him.

From there he went all the way back to Jerusalem. He wanted to join the disciples of Jesus in Jerusalem but they were terrified of him. They remembered how he had arrested many Christians and put them in prison and they thought it was a trap. The other Jews in Jerusalem still wanted to kill him and were trying to catch him. So the church in Jerusalem sent the Apostle Paul to Tarsus, which was a long way from Jerusalem.

Acts 9

Peter's Vision

One day the Apostle Peter was resting on the rooftop, waiting to eat. He was very hungry. Suddenly he saw a sheet coming down out of heaven. In the sheet were all kinds of animals that the Jewish people were not allowed to eat.

He heard a voice from heaven saying to kill and eat them. He was confused. God had forbidden Jewish people to eat this kind of meat, such as pork. Why would God tell him to eat it now? He answered and said, "But Lord, you know I've never eaten anything unclean." Then the Lord answered him and said, "If I decide food is clean, don't call it unclean." That was very confusing to Peter. He couldn't understand what this vision meant. Shortly afterward there was a knock at the door.

At the door was a Roman Soldier named Cornelius. He wanted Peter to baptize him as a Christian. Until now only Jewish people were Christians. He was the first Christian who was not Jewish.

Then Peter understood the vision: the Gospel is open to all people, not just to Jewish people. In Christ all are equal, Jews, Gentiles, men, women, people who are slaves or not. Acts 10

Peter & the Angel

The more the Apostles preached, the angrier the Jews got. Herod, the king, wanted to get rid of these Christians. They had succeeded in getting rid of Jesus. Now they wanted to get rid of Jesus' followers. He arrested James and Peter. He killed James and kept Peter in prison. He was guarded by 16 soldiers in prison! The Christians spent much time praying for him. They had lost the Apostle James. Now they didn't want to lose Peter as well. They were gathered together in a house praying all night about it.

Back in prison Peter was sleeping between two of the guards. He was chained and two other guards watched over him. Suddenly an angel stood next to him and light filled the jail cell. The angel told him to put on his shoes and clothes. The chains fell off his wrists. Peter hurried to do what the angel said and followed him. The guards were fast asleep. The gates of the prison opened by themselves as they came to them. Then when Peter was free the angel left. Peter went to the house where the Christians were gathered together. They were shocked to see him. Their prayers had been answered!

Acts 12

145

Paul & Barnabas

The Christians kept witnessing about the resurrection of Christ and the invitation to become part of the Bride of Christ. There were more and more people becoming Christians who were not Jewish. This was very confusing for the Christians who were Jewish. Remember that ever since the Ten Commandments and the law were given to the Israelites, they had been the only people God was working with.

But now, since Christ had come, everything was different. God was inviting people from every country, all over the world, to become a Christian and become part of the Bride of Christ. As the Jewish Christians started to understand this they decided they had to send the Apostle Paul to visit these new Christians. Remember when the Apostles received the gifts of the holy Spirit during the Day of Pentecost? They could give these gifts to other Christians as well through putting their hands on them. So, the Christians who had never met an Apostle did not yet have those gifts.

The church sent out the Apostle Paul and Barnabas to visit these Christians in distant places and give them the gifts of the holy Spirit. Back then, when they traveled they had to go every place either by walking or taking a boat. The Apostle Paul and his companion Barnabas, started out their trip. Acts 13

Paul Collects Money

As the Apostle Paul traveled among the Christians in Asia he met more and more who were Gentiles, or not Jewish. He had heard that there was a terrible famine in Jerusalem. So as he traveled he collected money everywhere he went for the Christians in Jerusalem who were suffering from lack of food. This was very important.

Do you think that God needed the Apostle Paul to do this? If the Christians did not give money to help their fellow Christians would God let them all starve? No, of course not. God will take care of His own people no matter what we do. But He wanted the Gentile Christians to have the privilege of helping the Jewish Christians. There was also another wonderful thing that happened. The church was united. The Jewish Christians in Jerusalem saw that the Gentile Christians in other places were willing to help them, even though they did not know each other. This showed them they were all part of the Body of Christ. They all had the same holy Spirit. They were all part of the same family. 1 Corinthians 16:1-4

Paul Casts Out a Demon

As the Apostle Paul traveled and preached, many people became Christians because of his teaching. He was a very powerful teacher. He convinced many people of the opportunity to follow Christ and receive the holy Spirit.

One day as he was walking to a place of prayer he met a girl who was possessed by a demon. Remember before the flood, when some of the angels disobeyed God and turned into human form? Well, these angels were no longer allowed to do this, but they were able to enter into people and make them do things they wanted them to do. This demon, or disobedient angel, was giving this girl the ability to tell the future. This can still happen today. That's why God wants us to have nothing to do with anyone who says they can tell us the future.

This girl was a slave of some very bad men and they were making alot of money from her. People would pay them to have her tell their fortune. The demons sometimes can guess the future.

Paul decided to cast this demon out of her so she could be free. When he did this the men who were her masters were very angry. They had Paul arrested, with his companion, Silas, and ordered them to be beaten. They accused them of creating a riot.

Acts 16

148

Paul & Silas in Prison

After Paul and Silas were arrested and beaten they were put in prison. That night they were heard by all the other prisoners singing hymns and praying to God.

About midnight there was a powerful earthquake. All the prison doors flew open and everybody's chains fell off. When the jailer realized what had happened, he took a sword and was going to kill himself. He thought Paul and Silas had escaped. When Paul saw this he shouted, "Don't hurt yourself! We are still here!" The jailer was so thankful that he fell down at their feet and asked what he should do to be saved. They told him to believe in the Lord Jesus Christ and he would be saved. He brought them back to his house that night and he and all the members of his family became Christians and were baptized.

The very next day the officials who put them in prison came and took Paul and Silas and requested for them to leave the city. Before they left the city they met with the other Christians there and encouraged them to be faithful.

Then they left that city and continued on in their travels. Acts 16

Paul Returns to Jerusalem

After much witnessing, preaching and convincing many people to become Christians, Paul returned to Jerusalem to see the Jewish Christians there. They were very thankful for the help they had received from the Gentile Christians every place the Apostle Paul had gone.

While he was in Jerusalem he went to the Temple to worship God. Because Paul had converted many Gentiles to become Christians many Jewish people thought he was against the Jewish Law given by God. This was not true. He still kept the Jewish Law himself. He did not teach Gentiles they had to live by the Laws given to the Jewish people. But he did not tell Jews they should no longer live by these laws.

But, while he was worshipping at the Temple in Jerusalem he was accused of bringing Gentiles with him, which was strictly forbidden. This was not true, but he was arrested by the Jews and put in prison. Once again the Apostle Paul was in chains! Acts 20:22-38

150

Paul Goes to Rome

The Apostle Paul had to go to Rome to stand trial before Caesar. The Jewish leaders in Jerusalem hated him, just like they had hated Jesus, and wanted to kill him. God had told him he must go to Rome to witness there and so, he was on a ship headed for Rome.

But on his way to Rome they passed through a terrible storm at sea. The ship they were sailing on broke into pieces in this storm. All the passengers, the Roman soldiers and all the prisoners were stranded on an island called Malta. They had to stay there for the whole winter until they could continue their journey to Rome after the winter was over.

While he was on this island the Apostle Paul was bitten by a poisonous snake, a viper. The people waited for Paul to die. When he was not poisoned by the bite the people on the island thought he was a god. He was able to heal many on the island that were sick and the people took good care of them all winter. After three months they were able to continue on their journey to Rome in another ship.
Acts 28:1-13

Paul Lives in Rome

When the Apostle Paul finally reached Rome, the Roman Christians were there to meet him and cheer him on along the road called The Appian Way.

Paul was not put in prison. Paul was allowed to live by himself with a soldier to guard him. He had his own rented house for two years. He did much preaching and witnessing from his own house. He asked the Jewish leaders to come so he could explain what he thought about Jesus Christ and preaching to the Gentiles.

Many people came to his house to hear him preach and became Christians. Because he could no longer travel he had time to do very much letter writing to the Christians he had converted in many places in the world. It's because of the Apostle Paul's writing of letters that we have most of the New Testament today.

Eventually the Apostle Paul was executed in Rome. We can read the tradition in history about this. Tradition tells us that he and the Apostle Peter died on the same day in the Roman persecution of Christians.
Acts 28:11-30

John the Last Apostle

The last Apostle living was John. He lived to be nearly 100 years old. During the Roman persecution of the Christians he was sent to live alone on an island called Patmos. There he had visions from God that he wrote down. These visions became the book of Revelation. It is a book of symbols. It tells, in symbolic language, the history of the Gospel Age, from the first Christians, until Christ returns to rule the Earth and to make the whole earth like the Garden of Eden once was.

During this Kingdom of Christ the faithful Christians who had believed and followed Jesus during the Gospel Age will reign together with Him. Remember, they will all be spirit beings. They will not become human once again. But, they will rule over the earth and take away all the sin and death.

There will be no more sickness, no more crying, no more pain, no more sorrow. All the sin and death that came from the disobedience of Adam and Eve in the Garden of Eden will be gone. And there will be no more Satan. He will be gone too. This is the time after the Gospel Age is ended. We call it the Millennial, or thousand year, Age.
Revelation 21:1-5

The New Testament is Done

When the Apostle John died the New Testament was finished. The last book, the Book of Revelation, was completed. Once the Apostles were gone the Christians had to depend on their teachings from what they had written. There were no more Apostles to lay their hands on other Christians to give them the gifts of the holy Spirit. Those gifts of speaking in tongues, healing, raising from the dead, all passed away.

But the most wonderful gift to the Christians today is the Bible. It has been written by hundreds of people since the book of Genesis was written thousands of years ago. God has made sure what we need to know about His Plan has been written down for us.

Because of this we understand the Plan of God and the future He has for us and all His creation. He has promised that through Jesus and His Bride, the Christians, He will bless all the people of earth. We also know that Christ will establish His Kingdom first in Israel. Israel is now being built again and will eventually be the capitol of the new Kingdom on earth.

Satan hates this Plan of God and does everything he can to attack God's people on earth, Christians, Jews or the nation of Israel. Zechariah 12 & 14

Gospel Age

From Jesus Baptized until the Church of Christ is Complete

God's Plan for Everybody

Everything we know about God's Plan comes from God's Word, the Bible. It is inspired by God. It tells us how sin and death came on the human race. It tells us how we will be delivered from it. The Bible gives us hope. It guides us. It tells us God's will for us.

God is still calling Christians to follow in the footsteps of Jesus. When that call is ended the new Kingdom of Christ will start on earth and all who ever lived will be raised back to life. They will have the opportunity to know what it is like to live under the rule of Jesus and His Bride, Christians. They will have the opportunity to change and follow God's will, to become perfect, in body, mind and character. Being perfect in character means they will only want to do what is right. They will not even want to do what is wrong. If they become perfect in character they will have the opportunity to live forever.

After the thousand years are over Satan will again be allowed to try and deceive the world. Those who follow him will die, this time for good. All those who do not follow him will be worthy to live forever.

This is God's Plan as He has revealed it to us in His Word. Because we know God's Plan and His Promises we know that the earth will not be destroyed. We know that God will finish the earth to be like the Garden of Eden. We know that all people will be raised from the dead and have an opportunity to live under the rule of Christ. They will have the opportunity to learn to do what is right, and not to do what is wrong. We know all those we love who have died will be awakened from the sleep of death. We will see each other again.

We pray every day from the Lord's Prayer:
Thy Kingdom Come, Thy Will be done on earth,
as it is done in Heaven! In Jesus' name, AMEN

Millennial Age

From Jesus' Return until
the World of Mankind is Perfected

God's Plan for Everybody

The Third World

The Millennial Age
From Jesus' Return until the World of Mankind is Perfected

The Second World

The Present Evil World
From the Flood until the Kingdom of Jesus Christ on Earth

The Gospel Age
From Jesus Baptized until His Church is Complete

The Jewish Age
From Jacob until Jesus is Baptized

The Age of the Fathers or Patriarchs
From the Flood until Jacob died

The First World

The World that Was
From the Garden of Eden until the Flood

From the Garden of Eden Lost until
the Garden of Eden Restored